The
AGE
of
MERCY

Overcoming religious conflicts
under the Supreme God,
EL CANTARE

RYUHO OKAWA

HS PRESS

Contents

1

Into the World Beyond Description

2

What is "Truth"?

3

For Peace and Love of the World

4

The Age of Mercy

Preface

You will find something "Great" in this book.

Yes, indeed, this is a book of Enlightenment, Love, and Mercy.

In this book, there are four speeches of mine.

However, to tell the truth, I received the revelations from Buddha and Jesus Christ.

But, truly, truly, I dare say, the Truth of this book is more than that.

You can see a slight figure of Spiritual El Cantare.

It is a true name of your God of this age and next age. It reveals who is real Allah. I am the "One". And I am the "All".

I'll bless you all.

Ryuho Okawa
Master & CEO of Happy Science Group
Sep. 17, 2019

1

Into the World
Beyond Description

January 30, 2009 at General Headquarters,
Happy Science, Tokyo

1

This World is Not Real

You are looking at illusions

"There is nothing in this world." If you hear these words, they might sound very strange. But, it is true. There is nothing in this world. Indeed, nothing. You are just looking at illusions. These are illusions. You are illusions. You, yourself, are an illusion. You misunderstand yourself. You have been misunderstanding. This is an illusion. This world is not stable. This world is a false world. This is not a real world.

Do you understand what I'm talking about? This is religion. This is faith. This is the meaning of real faith, real religion. Denying. It's the truth. To deny everything in this world. It's very important. You are apt to become attached to this world and everything in this world, but this is the origin of evil caused by your misunderstanding.

Your real self is light itself

Long long ago, you were angels. You were lights of Heaven. Very very old old days. I can't clearly say how many years have passed since then. But you have been, and really are now, angels.

But, you have misunderstood the truth about yourself and you have forgotten all of the truths. You, the real yourself, are light itself. But no one can imagine this truth because you are looking at illusions every day. You believe in what you see through your eyes, but this is the beginning of your misunderstanding.

This world is a tool to train your soul

This world is not a true world. It is false. If I can admit it a little, it's only a tool to train your soul. That is the meaning of this world. Almost all the beings in this world are false and illusions. Badness and illness arise from this illusion, this misunderstanding.

2

The Fact is Fact, the Truth is Truth

The believers of a false religion
Called science

You, yourself, are thinking that you are a body or a materialistic being. And nowadays, people who are very clever think that it is very cool to think in scientific terms. Everyone accepts this false belief easily. This false belief means that everything in this world can be explained in terms of a scientific situation. Why do such a lot of people believe in this false philosophy? I'm very sad about that. Science only has 200 or 300 years of history. Why are people apt to believe such kind of false religion?

We have been teaching real religion for more than a thousand years up to this century. In reality, beyond a thousand years, we have been teaching real religion. But you were defeated by false scientific religion in these 200 or 300 years. It's very sad.

Science leads to illusion, and people are attached to material things in this world. They think that this world is the only world and there is no other world. No exception. They think that only the things that they can touch are real beings, but this is an illusion.

Gautama Siddhartha already taught about this. He taught that it's misleading. It *was* misleading and it *is* misleading. People are liable to think and believe in their physical feelings, or some kind of reality they felt through physical things. And Gautama Siddhartha denied that.

Only chosen people can show the reality

Jesus Christ also always insisted, about 2,000 years ago, on the existence of the higher spiritual being in the air, and insisted that He is the real father of human beings. But he couldn't show his real father to all the people in the Middle East at that time. It's very difficult.

People in this world cannot see the real world. So, only the chosen people can show and teach these realities. But under a democratic way of thinking, a small number of people cannot persuade all of the remaining people. It's a very weak point of this period. Majority of people always think of themselves as right and the minority of people are usually disregarded and think they are wrong.

But truth is truth, fact is fact. We must conquer the tendency of this era, this tendency of this worldly democratic way of thinking.

The True Buddha is only born by one man, With one religion, in one age

In religion, the Truth is always spoken by one person. It's not democratic. Only one person can receive revelation from Heaven, I mean from

God or higher spirits. Only one person, in one religion, in one age. That is the True Buddha.

A True Buddha can only be born by one man, with one religion, in one age. There is only one who can teach the Truth for all people. There are now a lot of people in the world. We cannot count how many people are living in this world on Earth. But the Truth must be received only by one person.

This is not democratic. But when the people who believe in him become a majority, at that time, the remaining people would be influenced by them. And at that time, real faith just begins. So, it's very difficult to choose correct words, but we are living in a miserable world in a miserable period, for a real religious person.

A bad behavior of the mass media

People of the common sense usually appear as enemies. They cannot believe. In this age democracy is supported by many mass media. However, the mass media have one characteristic of bad behavior. It's that they have one policy or philosophy. This philosophy is, "Don't believe anything." It's a philosophy of theirs. They cannot believe and they want to reveal bad things or evils, and at that time, they believe that they can find reality or the truth. This is their habit.

But we, religious people, cannot show scientific proof to them. So usually, they cannot believe in religion. This is a difficult question.

We are just insisting on our Truth

But I'll say it again: The fact is fact, the truth is truth. We cannot be defeated by any powers or by any other false thoughts of the world. I don't know how many people believe in such kind of newspaper's truth or TV's truth. But we are just insisting on our Truth, the Truth which we believe in. It's very difficult.

So, I'll say it again: This world is a false world. This is an illusion. You are not yourself. You are not what you think you are. If you don't know the reality, the real teachings, or the basic teaching of the Buddha's Truth, to the least, you cannot know yourself.

3

What You Will Experience
At the Time of Death

Meeting your deceased relatives

Who in this world can believe that something which you cannot see is your reality? It's very difficult. For them, a soul is like air. A soul and air are equal to them, so they cannot believe.

People who believe in the existence of the mind often think that the mind is just a function of the brain. It's very sad. Doctors in this age who are very brilliant and clever think like that. I'm very sad.

I insist that people who are dead can now think, have emotions and can choose their own actions. This is very unfamiliar to doctors, but it's real.

When you are dying, you can see something you have never seen. That is your relatives who have already passed away. For example your grandfather, grandmother, or your father, mother, brother, sister, or friends who have already passed away. At the time of death you'll meet them.

Seeing another of you from above

After that, you leave your body and you can look down upon your own body on the bed in the hospital from the ceiling. At that time, you feel upset. "I'm here. Why is another one of me lying on the bed?" You'll be astonished. No one can explain about that. You have no knowledge about that. You have no education about that.

On the contrary, you are being taught by the mass media that, "The other world is false. Religious people are talking about evil things. They are misleading. They sometime make up teachings to earn money." And you believe in that.

After 24 hours, the silver cord will be separated
And you can go anywhere

But, when you leave your body, you will be upset and astonished by the fact that there are two of you. One is lying on the bed and another is in the air. At that time, you have a silver cord and the two bodies—one is the physical body and the other is of course the soul—are binded by the silver cord.

And about 24 hours later, the silver cord will be separated from you and at that time, you can go anywhere; You can go through the wall; You can go and fly through the air; You can fly over your city and look down upon all the scenes of the city. It's a very strange feeling, an incredible feeling. "What is this? What is this fact?"

At that time, you are apt to think, "I might be dreaming. It's a dream. It's a bad dream. Sometime I can get up and find that I was having a bad dream." But it will never come because a dream is truth and truth is a dream. Can you accept this paradox? A dream is truth, truth is a dream. This is a reality. This is the real teaching.

You would need time to accept this fact, but to accept this fact is the beginning of your enlightenment. At that time, you would gradually begin to know that, "Oh, I'm not the physical body. The physical body is not myself. It was my tool. Oh, I am the soul. What is this?"

The color of your clothes
Shows the tendency of your mind

At the time, when you look at yourself, you look like a human being. You are like a human being for the first 40 or 50 days. In Japan, China or Tibet, it is said to be 49 days. But for about two or three months, you will think that your style is almost the same.

You are a soul but you are wearing something. It's incredible. At first, you will be wearing what you wore when you were alive, attending school or going to your company. But after two or three months, your shape will change a little and you will be wearing another clothes; sometimes a blue wear, a white wear or a yellow wear, or something like that.

The color shows the tendency of your mind. For example, when you are in white clothes, it means purity or you are living with love for the people.

When you look at yourself and your clothes is blue, it means that your tendency is concentrated on knowledge. It means, you think that to be smart is a great thing. It means you are attached to knowledge or you think that educational background is very important in this age. In this case, you are such kind of person.

When you look at yourself and your clothes is yellow, it means that you are some kind of a religious person. Yellow represents gold. It means that you used to believe in God or Buddha in your old days in this world. Such kind of people will look at themselves and see that they are wearing yellow clothes.

And there are, of course, red clothes. Such people usually have the tendency to fight with other people or they are living in the overly competitive world. Sometimes they are soldiers, sometimes they got promotion in this world, in their company or in the profitable society. Or sometimes they were winners in their competition and got a lot of money. This is the meaning that their clothes are red.

And sometimes people who look at their clothes, they would be wearing silver-like color. It means they are scientists or doctors, or something like that. They have a habit of thinking analytically, so at that time, they will be wearing silver clothes.

And there are people who are wearing black wear. It means, of course, as you guessed, they are usually thinking of bad things. And their minds and their hearts are not clear and transparent, so black represents their hearts. And these people wearing black clothes are usually accompanied by small evil beings, and they are going to Hell. It's the usual case.

Another people are wearing green clothes. It means they have the tendency to love nature and some of them are farmers. Others are people who love landscape, beautiful places, rivers, mountains, flowers, butterflies, or something like that. People who love nature wear green clothes.

These are examples. There are a lot of different situations. But I just want to say that when you leave your body, you are wearing your usual clothes, but after two or three months, you are wearing one simple colored wear. It represents your mind tendency and it predicts your future. It's very strange.

You can go to other stars or galaxies

And in every case, you, yourself, have a spiritual body and the spiritual body can go through material beings, such as a wall, a building or a car, like that. You can go through every being in this world. And except some medium or spiritual person, when you speak to people in this world, they cannot hear anything. You can speak to them, but you cannot be heard by them.

You can go through everything in this world. You can even fly and dig deep into this Earth and go out from the other side of the Earth. It's possible. You need only five or ten minutes. It's a very strange and curious feeling.

After you've experienced a lot of spiritual activity in this world, you can leave this Earth and go to another planet or star. For example, you can fly to the Moon, go around the Moon and come back to Earth. Or you can go to Venus or other planets.

Sometimes you can go far away, from this galaxy to another galaxy. But to your astonishment, when you want to go to another galaxy from this galaxy, it only takes a few minutes. Only a few minutes.

There, you can see other human being-like creatures living and having a life. You will be astonished again that there are other kind of human beings. I'll talk about these universal beings again at another time. But this strange world is the real world.

4

To be a Real Human, You Need Belief

At the beginning of this story, I said to you that you live in a false world and you are looking at an illusion, just an illusion. It's the meaning of my story. OK?

So, if you want to know the real world and who you are, you need to have belief in real religion. Only belief can teach you these meaning and reality. So, through this title "Into the World Beyond Description," I want to teach you that you need belief. Everyone and everybody need belief. To be a real human, you need belief. This is the meaning of today's lecture.

2

What is "Truth"?

December 30, 2018 at Special Lecture Hall,
Happy Science, Tokyo

1

We Have Souls in Our Bodies

Today, I want to teach you a simple truth, especially regarding Buddhism.

This is a special lecture. It means, I wanted to go to Thailand in January, but there occurred several troubles on my way to Thailand. Mainly, it's a spiritual one. In reality, it's from the politics, the military administration, and the laws of Thailand. They are protecting themselves against the teachings of the real Buddha. So, I will send you the voice of Buddha. This is a Truth.

I do not know if you are educated in any way, are controlled under some sort of laws of modern society, or are under the authority of your king, but Buddha's authority is above them. So, I just really want to teach you a simple Truth, a simple Buddha's Truth. This is a Truth that I will teach you in very simple words, in a very simple way, and in a very simple meaning.

As you know, you human beings have souls in you. This is the reality. Some people do not believe in the existence of souls, for example, formally, the Chinese people or maybe the North Korean people. In reality, they each believe in the existence of souls, but formally or in a political meaning, they are prohibited from believing in the reality of the soul.

However, as you know, we have souls in our bodies. It's a simple but important Truth. The existence of souls is realized by Buddhism, of course, Christianity, of course in the Islamic teachings, in the old Jewish teachings, by the old oriental religions, the Egyptian religions, and the old European religions. They all recognized the existence of the soul. This is the original stream of world religions. There is no religion which does not believe in the existence of the soul.

2

The Salvation Needed
In the Ancient Age

But in the 19th century in Germany, Karl Marx and his friend Engels were born, and they made Communism. Communism is much influenced by the Old Testament, the origin of Christianity.

In the ancient age, people were very poor. The king and the people of high position around the king had a lot of money, but almost all the people were poor and suppressed by that power. So, in that age, God sent a message to the people of that age, "To be poor is not bad. To be poor is to be near God because God loves people who do not have enough and who are just seeking for the help of God."

Or in India or Nepal, poor people were seeking for the salvation of Buddha. Buddha and God are equal or not, you cannot say clearly, but Buddha, in the real meaning or the usual meaning, comes from the historical Buddha, I mean Gautama Siddhartha who was born more than 2,500 years ago in Nepal and made activities in India. He was a human in his activities with a great soul in him.

3

There are
Two Streams of Buddhism

But this kind of recognition about Buddha changed in the stream of ages. As you know, there are two streams of Buddhism. One is Theravada Buddhism. It is believed in Sri Lanka, Thailand, Myanmar, Laos, around there. A different Buddhism came from India through Central Asia, China, and Korea, and reached Japan in the sixth century. This Northern Buddhism is called the Great Vehicle Buddhism movement and sometimes Theravada Buddhism is looked down upon by them as the Small Vehicle Buddhism.

The reason is that Theravada Buddhism just thinks about oneself; it is just the seeking of the attainment of the individual. Of course, it is one part of the original Buddhism, but in reality, it is the former part of Buddha's activities, especially influenced by the first six years of spiritual training of Gautama Buddha.

In that age, Buddha was seeking for the Truth and was thinking about his attainment only, just focusing on his enlightenment. He was just thinking about how to get the enlightenment of himself. He had been seeking for six years. He left Kapilavastu Castle at the age of 29, struggled for about six years, and at the age of 35, he attained enlightenment.

At that time he thought, "I got the enlightenment. This enlightenment is a very difficult Truth to spread to the people of India." He thought, "It's over. My life is already complete and I can leave this world. My enlightenment is too difficult for people." So, he thought that he can complete his life and depart this world for another world, the heavenly world, or the Buddha realm.

But at the time, several Indian gods, or in the Western meaning great angels, came to him and asked him three times, "Please Buddha, please teach your Truth to the people of India and the world. People cannot understand your enlightenment, but if they can focus on their training, is there any possibility for them to get some kind of enlightenment or some part of enlightenment?" They asked him so.

Buddha agreed. "Yes, all people have the possibility of attaining enlightenment, so I will try. But I know it is also difficult to get enlightenment. They all have possibilities, of course. I can indicate the full moon in heaven or the night sky, but if they will each look at the full moon or not depends on them. I will indicate the Truth, but they, themselves, must see the moon through their own eyes. Only the people who make efforts to look at the moon in the sky can see the moon, what I have seen." He said so. This is just what Theravada Buddhism indicated.

And the Great Vehicle Buddhism. Buddha originally said that, "Everyone must make the effort to look at the moon." But the Buddhism which was taught in the later ages in India, China, Korea, and Japan was influenced by Jesus Christ's Christianity. It meant that their faith had lacked the meaning or the hope for salvation, so year by year they could not imagine the ancient Buddha's reality and Buddha's statue was built; the historical Buddha became from a human being to a God-like being in the spiritual meaning. They sought for Buddha's salvation, the same as the salvation of the Western society's Savior or God. The Western world's God saves the people, so the Great Vehicle movement of Buddhism also has the meaning of salvation.

4

Buddha is
One of the Branches of El Cantare

I dare say, in reality, what is the real Buddha's thinking? Historical Buddha means the Buddha who lived about 80 years in this world. In his days, he thought that originally, he was a bodhisattva who was seeking for enlightenment and after the great enlightenment, he became Buddha. He said, "My disciples, you also can become buddhas if you follow my path rightly." So, Theravada Buddhism, people who believe in this kind of Buddhism are sometimes misunderstood by Western people and of course other Buddhists that they are just seeking for the living-Buddha-like lifestyle and the attainment of enlightenment.

But now, I dare say this is the voice of

Buddha. These 2,500 years, Buddha has been in heaven. It's the highest heaven of this world. I indicated that it is the ninth-dimensional world in my book, *The Laws of the Sun*. In that area, there are other saviors, of course. For example, Jesus Christ, Moses, or others.

But now, I started and made activities of Happy Science. Happy Science is declaring that our real Buddha and real God is El Cantare. This is the first concept for the people of the world. They do not know El Cantare in the historical meaning.

I will teach you in a simple way. El Cantare is a core consciousness of Buddha. In this core consciousness, there is the Eternal Buddha, of course, and another part of the core consciousness of El Cantare is for example Alpha, as you have seen in *The Laws of the Universe -Part I*. Alpha was the beginning. He was the first God of this Earth. This was more than 300 million years ago. Next was Elohim, 150 million years ago.

He was born in the Middle East and became the origin of a lot of religions around the Middle East and Africa. There are these Alpha and Elohim, and now, I am called Ryuho Okawa, also one of the core consciousnesses.

Can you understand what I said? Please think about a Mandala-like spiritual picture. In the center circle, there was a core consciousness which was called Alpha, Elohim, or in another name, Allah, large-print God or Buddha, the Eternal Buddha.

You, Theravada Buddhists believe that the Buddha who left this world shall never return. In some meaning, it is true. They are core consciousnesses of El Cantare, so they almost never come down to this earth. I came down to this earth only two times, and now this is the third time. Almost 100 million years had passed between each rebirth.[*]

---

[*] The core consciousness of El Cantare had been reborn less than once every 100 million years, but His branch spirits have been reborn more frequently than that.

Around the core consciousness of the Eternal Buddha, or El Cantare, there are small-scale buddhas. They were called Saviors in Western society. So, this kind of buddha comes down to this earth, then almost 3,000 years pass, and after that he comes down to this earth again. But this is not the same person. This is the energy of the Eternal Buddha. The Eternal Buddha has small parts of energy around its core consciousness. So, some parts of them came down to this earth and saved people. This is the Truth.

So, I will not say that all of Theravada Buddhism is wrong. In some meaning, they are right. But in another meaning, they are not right. The historical Buddha who lived 2,500 years ago is still in heaven, but I, Ryuho Okawa is the same energy, same saving power, and one part of the power has come down to this earth. When one part of the power lives through the real body, its power can get a new character and a new name and become the new Savior or the new Buddha. This is the Truth.

So, the historical Buddha is, as you say, still in Nirvana, the ninth-dimensional world. I am one of the core consciousnesses of El Cantare. The historical Buddha is also one of the branches of the core consciousness of the Eternal Buddha, El Cantare. This is what Happy Science is insisting. Please believe in the real thinking.

5

Buddha's Enlightenment, The Western Way of Political System and Freedom

In the historical Buddhism, if you say "love," it is usually thought like the attachment-like love. You, human beings, usually think attachment as love.

But real love is not such kind of attachment. Real love is just to give. To give others your warm heart is the real love. This is not attachment. This is quite contrary to attachment. This is the same as Buddha's way to enlightenment.

Buddha's enlightenment meant how to forget about and detach yourself from the bondage to this flesh, the three-dimensional body. The three-dimensional body makes self-protection activities and such kind of self-protection activities lead to the no-soul or non-spiritual thinking. It just attaches to materialism.

So, we just think that Western love, the real meaning of Jesus Christ-like love is just like the Middle Way and the attainment of enlightenment. Buddha's enlightenment meant how to abandon your selfish love. Abandoning selfish love is real love, and this real love means God's love like Jesus Christ said. Buddha's enlightenment is almost the same.

In this context, we must know that real faith is to love God. To love God is to love Buddha. To love Buddha is to act like Buddha. To act like Buddha is "abandoning the self-realization only". It means to think that "real self-realization is to make other people happier and to make utopia in this world."

People are judged by their activities only. The caste system usually says, "If you did good things in the old days and are reborn on this earth, at that time, you get into the rich class, I mean the rich people, wealthy people, or powerful people. People who did bad things a lot become lower-side people, it means the poor people or people who do not have enough influence or rights."

This is the radical problem of the Western way of political system. Of course, Japan has adapted the same system. People can resort to the original right to vote to choose their politicians. It means people can make the decision who can be the leader or leaders of them, and if their leaders are bad or did evil things, they can change their leaders by vote. This is the fundamental of the Western way of political thinking.

This is based on freedom; freedom of speech, freedom of political activities, and freedom of religion. In some meaning, these mean the responsibilities of the individual people. Individual people have the responsibility to conduct these rights. So, it is not a revolutionary one. It is the original power.

6
God and Buddha Gave Everyone A Chance to be a Leader

People's souls came from the Original God or Primordial Buddha. Primordial Buddha's light became the core consciousness of Buddha and the historical Buddha. The historical Buddha said that, "The people who choose the deed Buddha did can walk the road to Buddha, the way to Buddha." It means, in political thinking, you can become leaders. You have rights for that.

But you must be judged by your deeds. If you have virtue and did enough good things to other people, you have the right to be chosen by other people, and if you did bad things and lost your virtue, you must come down to ordinary people. It means that your deeds in this age will decide your next life, I mean your future life when you will be reborn 200 years or 300 years later on this earth.

So, please think like that. Everyone has a chance to be a small buddha and everyone has a chance to be a leader. This is freedom; this is the meaning of Buddha's light in you.

I just taught you that all people have chances, but all people must be judged by their thinking and deeds. You will change your future and challenge against it to transform yourself into another position, another possibility. All people are equal in this meaning. This is not Communism. This is just the equality of chances. God and Buddha gave people the equality of making challenges. That is the real meaning.

I taught you regarding religious matter and political matter, "What is 'Truth'?" in simple words. Please believe in me. I have taught you for more than 2,500 years. I have taught you for more than 300 million years. Please believe in me. After that, you can judge by yourself what is good or bad, what is right or evil, and what is justice.

3

For Peace and Love of the World

December 23, 2009 at Shibuya Shoja,
Happy Science, Tokyo

1

El Cantare and the Essence of Worldwide Religions

A special lecture just before Christmas

Today is a special lecture because today is December 23rd. It's a bit earlier than Christmas, but it's the very time we must refer to the essence of Christianity. All over the world, there are a lot of Christian people, and they are waiting for some revelation from Jesus Christ. But only here in Shibuya Shoja, and of course other shojas where you can watch my lecture, you can hear the real will, intention, aim, and purpose of Jesus Christ. So, today is very important.

Today's theme is, "For Peace and Love of the World." This is a great title, so even Mr. President Obama (at the time of the lecture) cannot make a speech about "For Peace and Love of the World."

It's very difficult. Only a savior can give a lecture on this theme. So, I'll try about this content.

The hidden name of
The Real Father

First of all, you all must think about the birth of a savior. One or two months ago, you have already seen *The Rebirth of Buddha*, a very famous spiritual film in Japan. Even in Uganda in Africa, more than one million people have seen this film. I think *The Rebirth of Buddha* is likely to be known all over the world from now on, but this is just the first step, the starting point. My intention is above that. "The Rebirth of Buddha" is for the easy understanding of all Japanese people and foreign people, but my real intention is above that.

Some of you have already read in my book, *The Laws of the Sun*, that I'm El Cantare, but the name "El Cantare" has been hidden in the history of the human race, so this is the first time you correctly have known the name of your Lord and the name of the real Father, the living Father.

"The Father" taught about by Jesus Christ 2,000 years ago is El Cantare. But the name "El Cantare" has been hidden for these 2,000 years or more than 2,000 years. Some people knew His name as "the Supreme Being," just "El," "Almighty Light," or something like that.

But I daresay unto you, this is almost the first time for me to show my figure in front of you, have a human life, a humankind-like personality and the voice of a human, and stand like a Japanese in front of you. But this is not my real figure.

I am the law itself.
I am the rule itself.
I am the light itself.
I am the alpha, I am the omega;
I am the beginning, I am the ending.
I am the responsibility.

I am that I am.

This is El Cantare.

Integrating the discrepancies between religions

There are a lot of religions in the world, as you know, and each of the religions has its god or Buddha or something like that, a kind of supreme being. This is the origin of the war between religions in the world. There are a lot of gods, and the teachings of each of those gods are a little different. In some cases, they confronted each other, so there needs some kind of integration or combination.

I must combine those kinds of discrepancies. And beyond those kinds of discrepancies between religions, I must insist that religion is good. Religion is beautiful. Religion is splendid. That's what I want to say to you.

Please don't look at the discrepancies, defects, or short points of religions. Please sincerely look at the essence of religion. The essence of religion is "peace and love." This is the essence of the worldwide religions, the religions which cover this Earth. This is the main point.

The real meaning of peace and love
That humankind has forgotten

I came here to teach you, all of you, what is peace, what is love. You, humankind, have forgotten about the real meaning of peace and love. Now, then I'll teach you. I'll show you the real meaning. It's what I meant, what I wanted to say. In every religion, I have instructed and have been instructing, in these several thousands of years from the heavenly world, the founder of every religion.

Peace means, if you are children of God, please be kind to other people and have good relationship with them, beyond your nationality, beyond your color of face, beyond your language, or beyond the constitution of your country. Please make a good relationship among you. It is my hope.

Peace is produced from reliance. Please rely on other people, other humans, and please wish to make with each other a brighter future. Be kind to other people. Be kind to other nations. Be kind to the beings which are born on this Earth. I am the responsibility, or the power which feels responsibility for this Earth.

2

The Age of Miracle

Pollution in the minds of people
In the current age

Now, all the people in the world are talking about the environment of this Earth. The environment of the Earth is essential, of course, but I daresay you need something more and more essential than that. It is about the pollution of your minds, people's minds, the minds of people of all races. There is pollution in your minds. That "pollution" means the defect of belief, I mean, disbelief in God or Buddha.

Why can you not believe in supreme beings?
I dare say
This is a rare case, indeed.
I know about that.
It is a miracle of the world.
It is a miracle of the times.
It is a miracle of the age.
It is a miracle of the era of the 21st century.

I came here again.
I came here on earth again.
I haven't forgot my promise.
I came here, and I am now standing here.
I am now teaching you.

The essence of love

Two thousand years ago, in the western area which is called Israel now, I taught a lot of lectures through the mouth of Jesus Christ. For example, "Love each other," "I am the prince of peace," and "I am the being from the beginning." A lot of lectures are written in the New Testament.

So, I will again teach you. English is not my mother tongue, so it is not enough for me here to teach you my real meaning exactly, I mean 100 percent, but almost all of you can hear me about what I want to say. So, I speak in English.

I daresay
I am the love, itself.
Love means the being
Which breeds other people, breeds this world,
And breeds the relationship of
Human networks in this world.
To love is to breed.
To love is to let other people grow up.
To love is to help others to grow up.

Love is a power,
And the most influential power in this world.

If you understand
My words exactly
Or what I mean by "love",
Love is the essence of God,
Love is the essence of light,
And love is the aim of
Human lives in this world.
To love is to believe.
To believe is to live.
To live is to just know
What you are.

Please live a better life from now on
Because you are the sons and daughters of love,
The love of the planet,
The love from the celestial world,
The love from the Superior Being.
And you, yourself, have
Such sacred beings, sacred light in you.

Now is the time for forgiveness

Please believe my words. These are the words from heaven. These are not the words of a human. These are the words from higher, ninth-dimensional heaven. These are the words which create this world on earth, the meaning of the lives of human beings.

So, if you believe in me,
Do, act, and exist
As love behaves itself.
It's not so difficult.
Be kind to others.
Be kind to your enemies.

Please give forgiveness for your enemies.
Please forgive people who insulted you,
Who brought you sad feelings,
And who hurt you.
Please give love to the people who hurt you.
And love even such kind of people.
Love such kind of people
Until you hurt yourself.

If you don't like some people, in your life or now, as is often the case, you hate such kind of people, and you cannot forgive such people.

But this is the time. You must give forgiveness for such kind of people because you are looking at me now, because I'm forgiveness, itself. I came here, to this terrestrial world, to forgive people. I don't want to make you sinners. You are not sinners if you believe in me because I'm forgiveness, itself.

Aim for progress
And become closer to God

Men and women are likely to make mistakes,
And easily go into the way of decline.
However, here I am.
I am the progress.
I am the progress, itself.
I stand by you
To assist you to progress.
You must aim for progress.
Progress means to become a higher being,
To become more sacred,
To come to have a tendency to love God,
Or to be prone to stand by me.

3

"For Peace and Love of the Earth" —the Wish of God

Peace and love are brother and sister, Or sister and brother

So, by one day, a bit earlier than the usual Christmas celebration, I daresay... in reality, I must make a speech in front of the Christian people in church, but I am making a speech through Happy Science, in Shibuya Shoja, for the people who believe all over the world.

Today, my lecture, in a nutshell, is about peace and love. Peace and love are not different ones. Peace and love are sister and brother. Brother and sister, it's peace and love. Where there is love, there is peace. Where there is peace, there is love. Love and peace, peace and love, they are sister and brother, brother and sister. We cannot choose only one. We must choose both two.

Mr. President Obama of the United States has received the Nobel Prize regarding peace, but even now, he's bombing Afghanistan with some kind of reason, I know. In the standpoint of the United States of America, they cannot forgive terrorism or terrorists. I know about that.

But even the Taliban people, they, themselves, are not evil people. In their word, in their language, "Taliban" means "students of God." It means so in Islam. Even the Islamic teachings, I made influence on it in the history of humankind.

So, I must save people from hatred or misunderstanding of religions. If God doesn't like some race, I mean, some kind of nation, for example, their skin color is red, black, blue, white, or yellow, I don't know exactly but, it is not the real meaning, the real heart of God. So, I want to go further than the Nobel Prize and teach the real meaning of peace on Earth. It's made by reflection between two people who stand on different bases of religion.

I need people of light in countries
All over the world

So, Happy Science is very, very important in this time, in this era, in this global age of people. Only we, Happy Science, can integrate and can accept all differences of religions.

I need the people of light in this world. I need disciples who assist me in this age, in this world, in this country, and in your countries. Evil has been made by human beings. Now then, if this is the truth, evil almost can be destroyed, can be made to disappear from this Earth, by dint of human power and human beliefs.

I am the main light. However, I need different kinds of light from all over your countries. Not only the Japanese, but also the people from other countries can assist our movement, and of course, be invited to this movement because we are one, we are one nation, we are one race, and we are the children of the Supreme Being who are living in this globe.

So, be brave,
Be positive,
Be constructive,
Be patient,
And be kind to others.
People who obey my teachings
Will meet again in the near future,
In a beautiful landscape, the heavenly world.

You are now invited by God

I again tell unto you,
Peace and Love, Peace and Love,
These are required now, on this Earth.
Beyond the United Nations, we, Happy Science
Conduct this peace and love on Earth.

So, if there are first-timers in you,
Please believe in me.

I just came here
To save the people of the world,
Not just the Japanese people.
I am not the savior of the Japanese people.
I am the being beyond this country.
I love each of the people of every country.

So, believe in me.
Please follow me.
Do what you can, what you are able to do.
You are invited now.
God thinks that
You are available as tools of God,
To live as tools of God.
Be brave.
Be courageous.
And lead splendid lives.

Thank you. Merry Christmas.

4

The Age of Mercy

September 18, 2011 at Kuala Lumpur Convention Centre,
Kuala Lumpur, Malaysia

1

All Religions
Come from One Origin

A condition for Malaysia to become
An advanced country

Hello, Malaysia. Nice to meet you. Thank you very much for coming today. I'm very happy to meet so many people here in Malaysia.

This is my first lecture in Malaysia as announced already [*audience applauds*], but this might be the last lecture if you do not believe me [*audience laughs*]. So, these 30 minutes are very important. It depends on you. If this will be my first or the last time, I do not know exactly; Only God knows about that.

But I've heard you, Malaysian people, are very spiritual people. It's very welcoming for me, and a very good condition for me to give a lecture.

Recently I've heard that this country is aiming at becoming one of the advanced countries in the world by 2020. From the appearance of the city, this seems almost possible in the meaning of civilization, such as in the construction of buildings, in the construction of a lot of factories, and in the construction of modern utilities.

And also, I've heard that you are very spiritual people, and I was impressed by that.

But here in Malaysia, there is one condition that you must solve by 2020. It is about religion.

Even for me, it's very difficult to speak my own opinion strictly to you, because there are a lot of religions in the world and there are walls between each religion. So, it is my main aim to overcome this barrier between religions.

God's love is proved
By revelations from Heaven

Nowadays one of the main problems is the misunderstanding between the Western society—the Christian society of course—and the Islamic society. Muslim people are nowadays misunderstood, and even in this country, Malaysia, it's very difficult to deal with religious matters. It's very difficult, indeed.

But I dare say that all religions come from one origin. It is already said so in the Quran by Muhammad; he said "the One God sent Abraham, Noah, Moses, and Jesus Christ. He said that they are the messengers of God and that the last prophet is Muhammad."

I think this expression is interpreted a little differently by Western people. There is not much difference between a prophet, a messenger, and an envoy, but this expression is interpreted very strictly. This is one misunderstanding.

And I dare say, that is not all. The One God also sent Socrates of Greece, Confucius of China, Gautama Siddhartha of India, and other prophets and messengers from the heavenly world. There is the Supreme Being in Heaven.

Just as Muhammad received revelations from Heaven through Gabriel 14 centuries ago, I also received revelations this time in 1981. More than 30 years have passed since then. During these 30 years, I published more than 700 books and held almost 1,600 lectures.* This is the power of the Supreme Being. This is not the power of a human being.

The same thing happens in several hundreds or several thousands of years. This is the proof of the love of God. The love is proved by revelations from Heaven.

---

* At the time of the lecture. As of September, 2019, the author has published over 2,500 books and has given over 2,900 lectures.

2

Religion is not a Tool
To Rule People

**All people have the right to know
The real knowledge of God**

More than 60% of Malaysian people are Muslims, but in this place we publicized "Non-Muslims Only." I feel very sorry about that.

Yesterday I went to the Kinokuniya Bookstore near here. One Muslim lady was reading my book at the entrance.

I asked her, "Is it a good book? Are you interested in the book?" Then she said, "Yes, it's very interesting."

So I said, "Please look at the picture of the man on the cover of the book. It's me who wrote the book!" [*Audience laughs*]. She was astonished by that.

I believe discriminations and differences exist only in this earthly world. God does not want hesitation toward people. All people have the right to know, and the right to read the revelations and the real knowledge of God.

Religions should stand by people

I dare say: I was born as a Japanese this time. I'm Japanese, but in the accurate meaning, I'm not Japanese.

I am the national teacher of Japan now. For example, our new Prime Minister Noda (at the time of the lecture) has heard my lecture at our local branch, and he has studied my books. Also, Empress Michiko (at the time of the lecture) has been reading my spiritual books for more than 20 years. I'm established as a spiritual leader in Japan.

I started this new mission, the world missionary work, four or five years ago. And I found that people's races are not important; their religions are not important; their colors are not important; their opinions and creeds are not important. What is important is the meaning of religion; whether or not religions want to stand by people, or stand by each person.

In some countries, religion is used as a tool to rule people. It is misused as an explanation for poverty. Or, when the rulers do not succeed in economic growth, they ascribe it to religion.

But I am sure that religion should stand by people.

Look at the affairs occurring in Africa. Look at the incidents occurring in the Middle East. There are happening a lot of wars and conflicts, but they are not just wars and conflicts. They are wars between religions that are *for* the people and religions that are *against* the people. These are the phenomena occurring in the world nowadays.

3

El Cantare is the Last Hope of The Human Race

The Supreme Being exists
Beyond all gods

I dare say:

It's time; this is the time. This is the time that all of you were waiting for. This is the last chance for the people, the human race.

Now, seven billion people are living on earth, and the population is heading toward ten billion soon in this century. Now is the time. If the One God exists in Heaven, He must surely say something to the people of the world.

I said *He*, but He is not a human; He is the Supreme Being; the Supreme Being which exists beyond gods of all nations. There is the Supreme Being. Muhammad said it correctly; it's true.

But I dare say: Do not use God as a tool of war, a tool for triflings, or a tool for conflicts. God hates people killing each other. God loves people. The mercy of God is given through His revelations, through the messengers and prophets He sends.

In my book, *The Golden Laws*, there is written the secret project of God. There are a lot of messengers, envoys and prophets.

I dare say: Christian people say that Jesus Christ is the only son of God. In some meaning it's true, but in another meaning it's not true.

God sends a lot of angels, great angels, and near-God existences into this world for the love of the people, for the love of the world, and for the love of pacifism.

So, don't envy other people. Don't be angry about the differences between races and between people.

The God who appears in the Quran is El Cantare

The One Supreme Being was called El and sometimes Elohim.

In the Quran, the Only God sometimes says *I* and sometimes says *We*. *I* means El, and *We* means Elohim. Elohim means El Cantare; that is the truth.

I dare say:

I am the last hope for the human race.

I am the Gospel for the human race.

The time has come.

You need a new religion which combines all the religions and all the differences, and overcomes all the discriminations in the world.

Regardless of the color of skin, the differences in educational and academic background, the difference in wealth, or breeding, God loves every person. I dare say that nationalities mean nothing to El Cantare.

El Cantare can overcome every difficulty occurring on this earth. So, I came here.

4

We are Living in The Age of Mercy

We invited non-Muslims only to this place, but today, our members from Iran came here from across the sea. Dozens of our Iranian members came here to listen to my lecture, because it is very difficult for them to enter Japan due to the 9.11 incident. So, they came to Malaysia only to listen to me for 30 minutes. I think they are very blessed people. I love them.

I love Islamic people,
I love Buddhist people,
I love Christian people,
I love people of all other religions,
And of all nations.
I love the people who believe in me,
And I also love the people

Who do not believe me.
This is mercy.
This is the mercy which nourished
Human beings from the beginning.

I first appeared on earth 300 million years ago.
At that time, my name was Alpha.
I appeared again and at that time,
My name was Elohim.
Thirdly, I declared that the hidden name
Of the Supreme Being is El Cantare.

El Cantare means
The light of the Earth.
I am the creation itself.
I am the improvement of the human race.
I am the destination of the people in the world.
I am the key to Heaven.
And I am the forgiveness
For all of you.

Please overcome your difficulties.
Please overcome your sufferings.
Please overcome every past revelation
And the differences in religion.
You are children of God.
You are created equal.
You are promised to be
Happier and happier.
That is my real desire.

I dare say:
Each of you is equal.
At the bottom of your hearts,
You all have a diamond of God.
You and El Cantare, we are the same.
We are one.
Asia is one.
The world is one.
We are living in the Age of Mercy.

Mercy is a different name of God.
Mercy means,
"God stands by you every day.
In whatever case, come what may,
God is with you".
When God is with you,
Nothing can defeat you.
You can overcome everything.
You are invincible beings.
Please believe in me.

This is my message in Malaysia.
Thank you very much.

ABOUT THE AUTHOR

RYUHO OKAWA was born on July 7th 1956, in Tokushima, Japan. After graduating from the University of Tokyo with a law degree, he joined a Tokyo-based trading house. While working at its New York headquarters, he studied international finance at the Graduate Center of the City University of New York. In 1981, he attained Great Enlightenment and became aware that he is El Cantare with a mission to bring salvation to all of humankind. In 1986 he established Happy Science. It now has members in over 100 countries across the world, with more than 700 local branches and temples as well as 10,000 missionary houses around the world. The total number of lectures has exceeded 2,900 (of more than 130 are in English) and over 2,500 books (of more than 500 are Spiritual Interview Series) have been published, many of which are translated into 31 languages. Many of the books, including *The Laws of the Sun* have become a best seller or a million seller. Up to date, Happy Science has produced 18 movies. These projects were all planned by the executive producer, Ryuho Okawa. Recent movie titles are *Life is Beautiful – Heart to Heart 2 –* (documentary released Aug. 2019), *Immortal Hero* (live-action movie to be released Oct. 2019), and *Shinrei Kissa EXTRA no Himitsu – The Real Exorcist –* (literally, "The Secret of Spirits' Café EXTRA – The Real Exorcist –," live-action movie to be released in 2020). He has also composed the lyrics and music of over 100 songs, such as theme songs and featured songs of movies. Moreover, he is the Founder of Happy Science University and Happy Science Academy (Junior and Senior High School), Founder and President of the Happiness Realization Party, Founder and Honorary Headmaster of Happy Science Institute of Government and Management, Founder of IRH Press Co., Ltd., and the Chairperson of New Star Production Co., Ltd. and ARI Production Co., Ltd.

WHAT IS EL CANTARE?

El Cantare means "the Light of the Earth," and is the Supreme God of the Earth who has been guiding humankind since the beginning of Genesis. He is whom Jesus called Father, and His branch spirits, such as Shakyamuni Buddha and Hermes, have descended to Earth many times and helped to flourish many civilizations. To unite various religions and to integrate various fields of study in order to build a new civilization on Earth, a part of the core consciousness has descended to Earth as Master Ryuho Okawa.

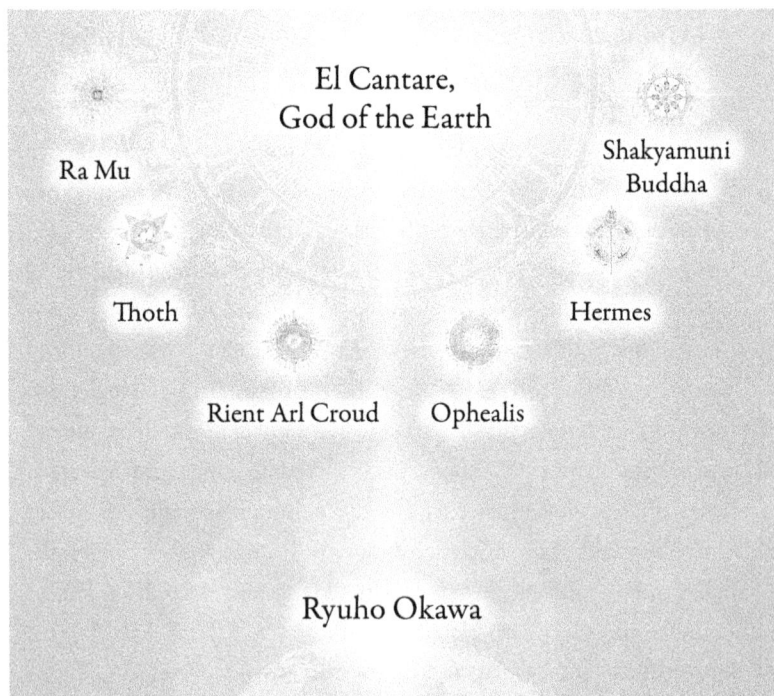

El Cantare,
God of the Earth

Ra Mu

Shakyamuni
Buddha

Thoth

Hermes

Rient Arl Croud

Ophealis

Ryuho Okawa

Shakyamuni Buddha
Gautama Siddhartha was born as a prince into the Shakya Clan in India around 2,600 years ago. When he was 29 years old, he renounced the world and sought enlightenment. He later attained Great Enlightenment and founded Buddhism.

Hermes
In the Greek mythology, Hermes is thought of as one of the 12 Olympian gods, but the spiritual Truth is that he taught the teachings of love and progress around 4,300 years ago that became the origin of the rise of the Western civilization. He is a hero that truly existed.

Ophealis
Ophealis was born in Greece around 6,500 years ago and was the leader who took an expedition to as far as Egypt. He is the God of miracles, prosperity, and arts, and is known as Osiris in the Egyptian mythology.

Rient Arl Croud
Rient Arl Croud was born as a king of the ancient Incan Empire around 7,000 years ago and taught about the mysteries of the mind. In the heavenly world, he is responsible for the interactions that take place between various planets.

Thoth
Thoth was an almighty leader who built the golden age of the Atlantic civilization around 12,000 years ago. In the Egyptian mythology, he is known as god Thoth.

Ra Mu
Ra Mu was a leader who built the golden age of the civilization of Mu around 17,000 years ago. As a religious leader and a politician, he ruled by uniting religion and politics.

What is a Spiritual Message?

We are all spiritual beings living on this earth. The following is the mechanism behind Master Ryuho Okawa's spiritual messages.

1 You are a spirit

People are born into this world to gain wisdom through various experiences and return to the other world when their lives end. We are all spirits and repeat this cycle in order to refine our souls.

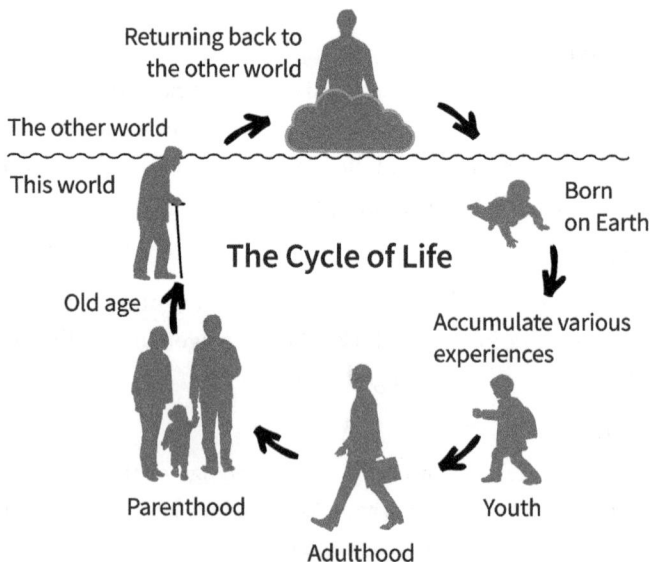

Returning back to
the other world

The other world

This world

Born
on Earth

The Cycle of Life

Old age

Accumulate various
experiences

Parenthood

Adulthood

Youth

2 You have a guardian spirit

Guardian spirits are those who protect the people who are living on this earth. Each of us has a guardian spirit that watches over us and guides us from the other world. They were us in our past life, and are identical in how we think.

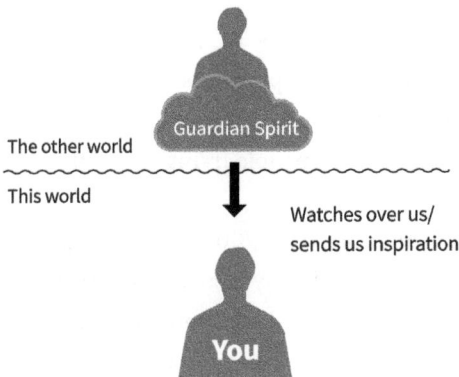

Guardian Spirit

The other world

This world

Watches over us/
sends us inspiration

You

3 How spiritual messages work

Master Ryuho Okawa, through his enlightenment, is capable of summoning any spirit from anywhere in the world, including the spirit world.

Master Okawa's way of receiving spiritual messages is fundamentally different from that of other psychic mediums who undergo trances and are thereby completely taken over by the spirits they are channeling.

Master Okawa's attainment of a high level of enlightenment enables him to retain full control of his consciousness and body throughout the duration of the spiritual message. To allow the spirits to express their own thoughts and personalities freely, however, Master Okawa usually softens the dominancy of his consciousness. This way, he is able to keep his own philosophies out of the way and ensure that the spiritual messages are pure expressions of the spirits he is channeling.

Since guardian spirits think at the same subconscious level as the person living on earth, Master Okawa can summon the spirit and find out what the person on earth is actually thinking. If the person has already returned to the other world, the spirit can give messages to the people living on earth through Master Okawa.

Since 2009, more than 700 sessions of spiritual messages have been openly recorded by Master Okawa, and the majority of these have been published. Spiritual messages from the guardian spirits of people living today such as Donald Trump, Japanese Prime Minister Shinzo Abe and Chinese President Xi Jinping, as well as spiritual messages sent from the spirit world by Jesus Christ, Muhammad, Thomas Edison, Mother Teresa, Steve Jobs and Nelson Mandela are just a tiny pack of spiritual messages that were published so far.

Domestically, in Japan, these spiritual messages are being read by a wide range of politicians and mass media, and the high-level contents of these books are delivering an impact even more on politics, news and public opinion. In recent years, there have been spiritual messages recorded in English, and English translations are being done on the spiritual messages given in Japanese. These have been published overseas, one after another, and have started to shake the world.

1 The guardian spirit / spirit in the other world...

2 Goes inside Master Okawa in this world

3 Master Okawa speaks the words of the guardian spirit / spirit

For more about spiritual messages and a complete list of books in the Spiritual Interview Series, visit **okawabooks.com**

ABOUT HAPPY SCIENCE

Happy Science is a global movement that empowers individuals to find purpose and spiritual happiness and to share that happiness with their families, societies, and the world. With more than twelve million members around the world, Happy Science aims to increase awareness of spiritual truths and expand our capacity for love, compassion, and joy so that together we can create the kind of world we all wish to live in.

Activities at Happy Science are based on the Principles of Happiness (Love, Wisdom, Self-Reflection, and Progress). These principles embrace worldwide philosophies and beliefs, transcending boundaries of culture and religions.

Love teaches us to give ourselves freely without expecting anything in return; it encompasses giving, nurturing, and forgiving.

Wisdom leads us to the insights of spiritual truths, and opens us to the true meaning of life and the will of God (the universe, the highest power, Buddha).

Self-Reflection brings a mindful, nonjudgmental lens to our thoughts and actions to help us find our truest selves—the essence of our souls—and deepen our connection to the highest power. It helps us attain a clean and peaceful mind and leads us to the right life path.

Progress emphasizes the positive, dynamic aspects of our spiritual growth—actions we can take to manifest and spread happiness around the world. It's a path that not only expands our soul growth, but also furthers the collective potential of the world we live in.

PROGRAMS AND EVENTS

The doors of Happy Science are open to all. We offer a variety of programs and events, including self-exploration and self-growth programs, spiritual seminars, meditation and contemplation sessions, study groups, and book events.

Our programs are designed to:
* Deepen your understanding of your purpose and meaning in life
* Improve your relationships and increase your capacity to love unconditionally
* Attain peace of mind, decrease anxiety and stress, and feel positive
* Gain deeper insights and a broader perspective on the world
* Learn how to overcome life's challenges
  ... and much more.

INTERNATIONAL SEMINARS

Each year, friends from all over the world join our international seminars, held at our faith centers in Japan. Different programs are offered each year and cover a wide variety of topics, including improving relationships, practicing the Eightfold Path to enlightenment, and loving yourself, to name just a few.

Happy Science official website

Happy Science's official website introduces the organization's founder and CEO, Ryuho Okawa, as well as Happy Science teachings, books, lectures, temples, the latest news, and more.

happy-science.org

Happy Science regularly publishes various magazines for readers around the world. The Happy Science Monthly, which now spans over 300 issues, contains Master Okawa's latest lectures, words of wisdom, stories of remarkable life-changing experiences, world news, and much more to guide members and their friends to a happier life. This is available in many other languages, including Portuguese, Spanish, French, German, Chinese, and Korean. Happy Science Basics, on the other hand, is a 'theme-based' booklet made in an easy-to-read style for those new to Happy Science, which is also ideal to give to friends and family. You can pick up the latest issues from Happy Science, subscribe to have them delivered (see our contacts page) or view them online.*

* Online editions of the *Happy Science Monthly* and
Happy Science Basics can be viewed at:
info.happy-science.org/category/magazines/

OUR ACTIVITIES

Happy Science does other various activities to provide support for those in need.

◆ **You Are An Angel!**
General Incorporated Association
Happy Science has a volunteer network in Japan that encourages and supports children with disabilities as well as their parents and guardians.

◆ **Never Mind School for Truancy**
At 'Never Mind,' we support students who find it very challenging to attend schools in Japan. We also nurture their self-help spirit and power to rebound against obstacles in life based on Master Okawa's teachings and faith.

◆ **"Prevention against suicide" campaign since 2003**
A nationwide campaign to reduce suicides; over 20,000 people commit suicide every year in Japan. "The Suicide Prevention Website-Words of Truth for You-" presents spiritual prescriptions for worries such as depression, lost love, extramarital affairs, bullying and work-related problems, thereby saving many lives.

◆ **Support for anti-bullying campaigns**
Happy Science provides support for a group of parents and guardians, Network to Protect Children from Bullying, a general incorporated foundation launched in Japan to end bullying, including those that can even be called a criminal offense. So far, the network received more than 5,000 cases and resolved 90% of them.

DOCUMENTARY MOVIE
HEART TO HEART

In this documentary movie, Happy Science University students visit these NPO activities to discover what salvation truly is, and on the meaning of life, through heart to heart interviews.

◆ **The Golden Age Scholarship**

This scholarship is granted to students who can contribute greatly and bring a hopeful future to the world.

◆ **Success No.1**
Buddha's Truth Afterschool Academy

Happy Science has over 180 classrooms throughout Japan and in several cities around the world that focus on afterschool education for children. The education focuses on faith and morals in addition to supporting children's school studies.

◆ **Angel Plan V**

For children under the age of kindergarten, Happy Science holds classes for nurturing healthy, positive, and creative boys and girls.

◆ **Future Stars Training Department**

The Future Stars Training Department was founded within the Happy Science Media Division with the goal of nurturing talented individuals to become successful in the performing arts and entertainment industry.

◆ **New Star Production Co., Ltd.**
ARI Production Co., Ltd.

We have companies to nurture actors and actresses, artists, and vocalists. They are also involved in film production.

MOVIES

HOPE LIVES FOREVER

IMMORTAL HERO

NEW MOVIE COMING SOON!

BASED ON THE TRUE STORY OF A MAN
WHOSE NEAR DEATH EXPERIENCE INSPIRES HIM
TO CHOOSE LIFE... AND CHANGE THE LIVES OF MILLIONS

Story

Makoto Mioya, a highly successful Japanese author and publisher, has a life-threatening, near-death experience. Powerful spiritual beings with whom he has communicated most of his adult life visit Makoto to remind him he has the power within to heal himself. Reborn, Makoto commits his life to sharing the almighty wisdom he receives from the spiritual realm. As doubters, including some of his own family, challenge and question his new-found ardor, Makoto must find a way to connect with his family and the 'family of man' to inspire a better world.

22 Awards from 6 Countries!

SPAIN BARCELONA INTERNATIONAL FILM FESTIVAL 2019 [THE CASTELL AWARDS]	**SPAIN** MADRID INTERNATIONAL FILM FESTIVAL 2019 [BEST DIRECTOR OF A FOREIGN LANGUAGE FEATURE FILM]
ITALY DIAMOND FILM AWARDS JUL 2019 [WINNER (NARRATIVE FEATUREFILM)]	**ITALY** FLORENCE FILM AWARDS JUL 2019 [HONORABLE MENTION: FEATURE FILM]
USA INDIE VISIONS FILM FESTIVAL JUL 2019 [WINNER (NARRATIVE FEATURE FILM)]	**ITALY** FLORENCE FILM AWARDS JUL 2019 [BEST ORIGINAL SCREENPLAY]

...and more!

For more information, visit **www.immortal-hero.com**

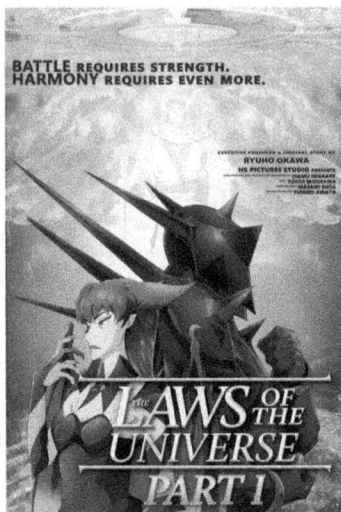

BATTLE REQUIRES STRENGTH.
HARMONY REQUIRES EVEN MORE.

THE LAWS OF THE UNIVERSE PART I

Up to date, Happy Science has produced 18 movies. These projects were all planned by the executive producer, Ryuho Okawa. Our movies have received various awards and recognition around the world.

....

The animation movie, *The Laws of the Universe – Part I*, released simultaneously in Japan and the U.S. in October 2018, has received a total of 5 awards from 4 countries (as of May, 2019). We thank you all for your support, and we wish that this movie can spread even more and people can discover this one and only Truth taught at Happy Science.

5 Awards from 4 Countries!

France
on May 18th

NICE INTERNATIONAL FILM FESTIVAL 2019
BEST INTERNATIONAL ANIMATION AWARD

U.K.
on May 25th

LONDON INTERNATIONAL MOTION PICTURE AWARDS 2019
BEST INTERNATIONAL ANIMATION FEATURE FILM AWARD

India

CALCUTTA INTERNATIONAL CULT FILM FESTIVAL
[OUTSTANDING ACHIEVEMENT AWARD]

U.S.

FILM INVASION LOS ANGELES
[GRAND JURY PRIZE – BEST ANIME FEATURE]

AWARENESS FILM FESTIVAL
[SPECIAL JURY ANIMATION AWARD]

Lineup of Happy Science Movies

Discover the spiritual world you have never seen and
Come close to the Heart of God through these movies.

•1994•
The Terrifying Revelations
of Nostradamus
(Live-action)

•2016•
I'm Fine, My Angel
(Live-action)

•1997•
Love Blows Like the Wind
(Animation)

•2017•
The World We Live In
(Live-action)

•2000•
The Laws of the Sun
(Animation)

•2018•
Heart to Heart
(Documentary)

•2003•
The Golden Laws
(Animation)

•2018•
DAYBREAK
(Live-action)

•2006•
The Laws of Eternity
(Animation)

•2018•
The Laws of the Universe - Part I
(Animation)

•2009•
The Rebirth of Buddha
(Animation)

•2019•
The Last White Witch
(Live-action)

•2012•
The Final Judgement
(Live-action)

•2019•
Life is Beautiful
- Heart to Heart 2 -
(Documentary)

•2012•
The Mystical Laws
(Animation)

—— Coming Soon ——

•2015•
The Laws of the Universe - Part 0
(Animation)

•2019•
Immortal Hero
(Live-action)

Contact your nearest local branch for more information on how to watch HS movies.

CONTACT INFORMATION

Happy Science is a worldwide organization with faith centers around the globe. For a comprehensive list of centers, visit the worldwide directory at *happy-science.org*. The following are some of the many Happy Science locations:

UNITED STATES AND CANADA

New York
79 Franklin St.,
New York, NY 10013
Phone: 212-343-7972
Fax: 212-343-7973
Email: ny@happy-science.org
Website: happyscience-na.org

San Francisco
525 Clinton St.,
Redwood City, CA 94062
Phone & Fax: 650-363-2777
Email: sf@happy-science.org
Website: happyscience-na.org

New Jersey
725 River Rd, #102B,
Edgewater, NJ 07020
Phone: 201-313-0127
Fax: 201-313-0120
Email: nj@happy-science.org
Website: happyscience-na.org

Los Angeles
1590 E. Del Mar Blvd.,
Pasadena, CA 91106
Phone: 626-395-7775
Fax: 626-395-7776
Email: la@happy-science.org
Website: happyscience-na.org

Florida
5208 8thSt., Zephyrhills,
FL 33542
Phone: 813-715-0000
Fax: 813-715-0010
Email: florida@happy-science.org
Website: happyscience-na.org

Orange County
10231 Slater Ave. #204
Fountain Valley, CA 92708
Phone: 714-745-1140
Email: oc@happy-science.org
Website: happyscience-na.org

Atlanta
1874 Piedmont Ave. NE, Suite 360-C
Atlanta, GA 30324
Phone: 404-892-7770
Email: atlanta@happy-science.org
Website: happyscience-na.org

San Diego
7841 Balboa Ave., Suite #202
San Diego, CA 92111
Phone: 619-381-7615
Fax: 626-395-7776
E-mail: sandiego@happy-science.org
Website: happyscience-na.org

Hawaii
Phone: 808-591-9772
Fax: 808-591-9776
Email: hi@happy-science.org
Website: happyscience-na.org

Toronto
845 The Queensway
Etobicoke, ON M8Z 1N6 Canada
Phone: 1-416-901-3747
Email: toronto@happy-science.org
Website: happy-science.ca

Kauai
4504 Kukui Street.,
Dragon Building Suite 21,
Kapaa, HI 96746
Phone: 808-822-7007
Fax: 808-822-6007
Email: kauai-hi@happy-science.org
Website: happyscience-na.org

Vancouver
#212-2609 East 49th Avenue
Vancouver, BC, V5S 1J9, Canada
Phone: 1-604-437-7735
Fax: 1-604-437-7764
Email: vancouver@happy-science.org
Website: happy-science.ca

INTERNATIONAL

Tokyo
1-6-7 Togoshi, Shinagawa
Tokyo, 142-0041 Japan
Phone: 81-3-6384-5770
Fax: 81-3-6384-5776
Email: tokyo@happy-science.org
Website: happy-science.org

Sydney
516 Pacific Hwy, Lane Cove North,
NSW 2066, Australia
Phone: 61-2-9411-2877
Fax: 61-2-9411-2822
Email: sydney@happy-science.org
Website: happyscience.org.au

London
3 Margaret St.
London,W1W 8RE United Kingdom
Phone: 44-20-7323-9255
Fax: 44-20-7323-9344
Email: eu@happy-science.org
Website: happyscience-uk.org

South Sao Paulo
Rua. Domingos de Morais 1154,
Vila Mariana, Sao Paulo
SP-CEP 04010-100, Brazil
Phone: 55-11-5574-0054
Fax: 55-11-5088-3806
Email: sp_sul@happy-science.org
Website: happyscience.com.br

Jundiai
Rua Congo, 447, Jd. Bonfiglioli
Jundiai-CEP, 13207-340, Brazil
Phone: 55-11-4587-5952
Email: jundiai@happy-science.org

Uganda
Plot 877 Rubaga Road, Kampala
P.O. Box 34130, Kampala, Uganda
Phone: 256-79-3238-002
Email: uganda@happy-science.org

Seoul
74, Sadang-ro 27-gil,
Dongjak-gu, Seoul, Korea
Phone: 82-2-3478-8777
Fax: 82-2- 3478-9777
Email: korea@happy-science.org

Thailand
19 Soi Sukhumvit 60/1,
Bang Chak, Phra Khanong,
Bangkok, 10260 Thailand
Phone: 66-2-007-1419
Email: bangkok@happy-science.org
Website: happyscience-thai.org

Taipei
No. 89, Lane 155, Dunhua N. Road.,
Songshan District, Taipei City 105,
Taiwan
Phone: 886-2-2719-9377
Fax: 886-2-2719-5570
Email: taiwan@happy-science.org

Indonesia
Darmawangsa
Square Lt. 2 No. 225
Jl. Darmawangsa VI & IX
Indonesia
Phone: 021-7278-0756
Email: indonesia@happy-science.org

Malaysia
No 22A, Block 2, Jalil Link Jalan
Jalil Jaya 2, Bukit Jalil 57000, Kuala
Lumpur, Malaysia
Phone: 60-3-8998-7877
Fax: 60-3-8998-7977
Email: malaysia@happy-science.org
Website: happyscience.org.my

Philippines Taytay
LGL Bldg, 2nd Floor,
Kadalagaham cor,
Rizal Ave. Taytay,
Rizal, Philippines
Phone: 63-2-5710686
Email: philippines@happy-science.org

Nepal
Kathmandu Metropolitan City
Ward No. 15, Ring Road, Kimdol,
Sitapaila Kathmandu, Nepal
Phone: 977-1-427-2931
Email: nepal@happy-science.org

ABOUT IRH PRESS

IRH Press Co., Ltd, based in Tokyo, was founded in 1987 as a publishing division of Happy Science. IRH Press publishes religious and spiritual books, journals, magazines and also operates broadcast and film production enterprises. For more information, visit *okawabooks.com*.

Follow us on:

Facebook: Okawa Books　　**Twitter**: Okawa Books

Goodreads: Ryuho Okawa　　**Instagram**: OkawaBooks

Pinterest: Okawa Books

RYUHO OKAWA'S LAWS SERIES

The Laws Series is an annual volume of books that are mainly comprised of Ryuho Okawa's lectures on various topics that highlight principles and guidelines for the activities of Happy Science every year. *The Laws of the Sun*, the first publication of the Laws Series, ranked in the annual best-selling list in Japan in 1994. Since then, all of the Laws Series' titles have ranked in the annual best-selling list for more than two decades, setting socio-cultural trends in Japan and around the world.

THE TRILOGY

The first three volumes of the Laws Series, *The Laws of the Sun*, *The Golden Laws*, and *The Nine Dimensions* make a trilogy that completes the basic framework of the teachings of God's Truths. *The Laws of the Sun* discusses the structure of God's Laws, *The Golden Laws* expounds on the doctrine of time, and *The Nine Dimensions* reveals the nature of space.

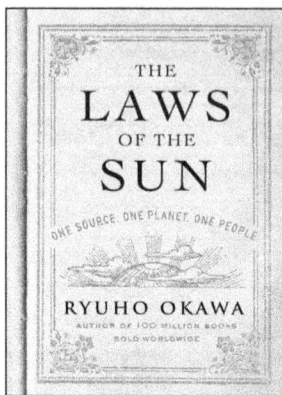

THE LAWS OF THE SUN
ONE SOURCE, ONE PLANET, ONE PEOPLE

Paperback • 288 pages • $15.95
ISBN: 978-1-942125-43-3

IMAGINE IF YOU COULD ASK GOD why He created this world and what spiritual laws He used to shape us—and everything around us. If we could understand His designs and intentions, we could discover what our goals in life should be and whether our actions move us closer to those goals or farther away.

At a young age, a spiritual calling prompted Ryuho Okawa to outline what he innately understood to be universal truths for all humankind. In *The Laws of the Sun*, Okawa outlines these laws of the universe and provides a road map for living one's life with greater purpose and meaning.

In this powerful book, Ryuho Okawa reveals the transcendent nature of consciousness and the secrets of our multidimensional universe and our place in it. By understanding the different stages of love and following the Buddhist Eightfold Path, he believes we can speed up our eternal process of development. *The Laws of the Sun* shows the way to realize true happiness—a happiness that continues from this world through the other.

*For a complete list of books, visit **okawabooks.com***

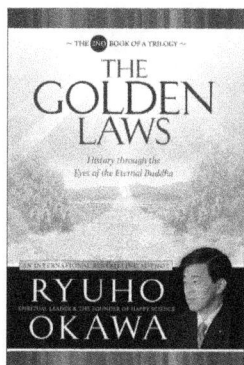

THE GOLDEN LAWS

HISTORY THROUGH THE EYES OF THE ETERNAL BUDDHA

Paperback • 216 pages • $14.95
ISBN: 978-1-941779-81-1

Throughout history, Great Guiding Spirits of Light have been present on Earth in both the East and the West at crucial points in human history to further our spiritual development. *The Golden Laws* reveals how Divine Plan has been unfolding on Earth, and outlines 5,000 years of the secret history of humankind. Once we understand the true course of history, through past, present and into the future, we cannot help but become aware of the significance of our spiritual mission in the present age.

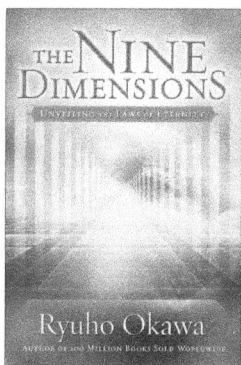

THE NINE DIMENSIONS

UNVEILING THE LAWS OF ETERNITY

Paperback • 168 pages • $15.95
ISBN: 978-0-982698-56-3

This book is a window into the mind of our loving God, who designed this world and the vast, wondrous world of our afterlife as a school with many levels through which our souls learn and grow. When the religions and cultures of the world discover the truth of their common spiritual origin, they will be inspired to accept their differences, come together under faith in God, and build an era of harmony and peaceful progress on Earth.

---

*For a complete list of books, visit **okawabooks.com***

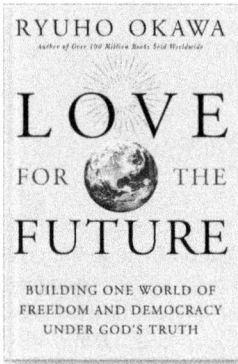

Love for the Future

Building One World of Freedom and Democracy Under God's Truth

Paperback • 312 pages • $15.95
ISBN: 978-1-942125-60-0

This is a compilation of select international lectures given by Ryuho Okawa during his (ongoing) global missionary tours. While conflicting values of justice exists, this book espouses that freedom and democracy are vital principles for global unification that will resolutely foster peace and shared prosperity, if adopted universally.

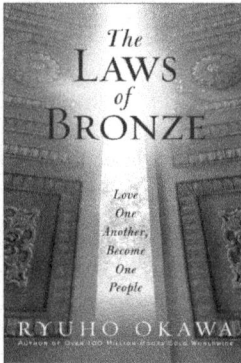

The Laws of Bronze

Love One Another, Become One People

Paperback • 224 pages • $15.95
ISBN: 978-1-942125-50-1

This is the 25th volume of the Laws Series by Ryuho Okawa. This latest volume will help the readers deepen their faith and elevate their awareness to a global scale and even to the cosmic level. This miraculous and inspiring book will show the keys to living a spiritual life of truth regardless of their age, gender, or race.

*For a complete list of books, visit **okawabooks.com***

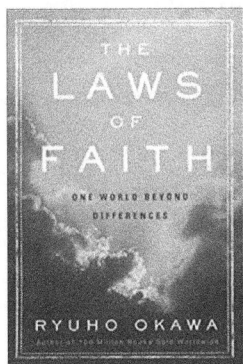

The Laws of Faith

One World Beyond Differences

Paperback • 208 pages • $15.95
ISBN: 978-1-942125-34-1

Ryuho Okawa preaches at the core of a new universal religion from various angles while integrating logical and spiritual viewpoints in mind with current world situations. This book offers us the key to accept diversities beyond differences in ethnicity, religion, race, gender, descent, and so on, harmonize the individuals and nations and create a world filled with peace and prosperity.

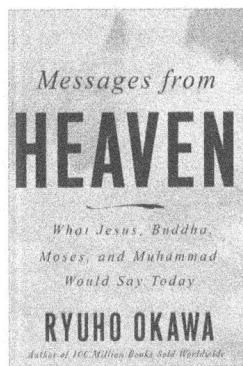

Messages from Heaven

What Jesus, Buddha, Moses, and Muhammad Would Say Today

Hardcover • 214 pages • $19.95
ISBN: 978-1-941779-19-4

If you could speak to Jesus, Buddha, Moses, or Muhammad, what would you ask? In *Messages from Heaven: What Jesus, Buddha, Moses, and Muhammad Would Say Today*, Ryuho Okawa uses his spiritual power to communicate with these four spirits and shares their messages to the people living today.

---

*For a complete list of books, visit **okawabooks.com***

*For a complete list of books, visit **okawabooks.com***

www.ingramcontent.com/pod-product-compliance
Lightning Source LLC
Chambersburg PA
CBHW021533260326
41914CB00001B/6